BAMBOO

Nature's FRIENDS

T0031269

by Joyce Markovics

NORWOOD HOUSE PRESS

NORWOOD HOUSE PRESS

For more information about Norwood House Press, please visit our website at: www.norwoodhousepress.com or call 866-565-2900.

Book Designer: Ed Morgan
Editorial and Production: Bowerbird Books

Photo Credits: David Clode/Unsplash.com, cover; flickr, title page; freepik.com, 4; Daniel Maissan/Unsplash.com, 5; © iStock.com/Khlongwangchao, 6; freepik.com, 7 top; Wikimedia Commons, 7 bottom; freepik.com, 8; Kathleen Franklin/flickr, 9; Wikimedia Commons, 11; Joi Ito/flickr, 12; freepik.com, 13; Jason Leung/Unsplash.com, 14; © iStock.com/doji1989, 15; Mark Stevens/flickr, 16 top; Anastasiia Rozumna/Unsplash.com, 16 bottom; freepik.com, 17; Charles Deluvio/Unsplash.com, 17 bottom; © iStock.com/PhotoTalk, 18; freepik.com, 19; Ricardo Gomez Angel/Unsplash.com, 20; freepik.com, 21; freepik.com, 23; freepik.com, 24; Rod Waddington/flickr, 25; Adam Dillon/Unsplash.com, 27; freepik.com, 29.

Hardcover ISBN: 978-1-68450-768-9
Paperback ISBN: 978-1-68404-775-8

Library of Congress Cataloging-in-Publication Data

Names: Markovics, Joyce L., author.
Title: Bamboo / by Joyce Markovics.
Description: Chicago : Norwood House Press, [2023] | Series: Nature's
   friends | Includes bibliographical references and index. | Audience:
   Grades 2-3
Identifiers: LCCN 2021057766 (print) | LCCN 2021057767 (ebook) | ISBN
   9781684507689 (hardcover) | ISBN 9781684047758 (paperback) | ISBN
   9781684047819 (ebook)
Subjects: LCSH: Bamboo--Juvenile literature.
Classification: LCC QK495.G74 M33 2023 (print) | LCC QK495.G74 (ebook) |
   DDC 584/.922--dc23/eng/20211217
LC record available at https://lccn.loc.gov/2021057766
LC ebook record available at https://lccn.loc.gov/2021057767

353N—082022

Manufactured in the United States of America in North Mankato, Minnesota.

CONTENTS

MIRACLE BAMBOO

In northern Ecuador, there's an emerald-green forest. It's not filled with trees, though. It's filled with treelike grasses called bamboo! Bamboo leaves cover the ground like a carpet. Nearby is a river. The family who owns the land calls it *El Milagro*. That's Spanish for "the miracle." The bamboo plants have changed their land—and their lives.

Cattle grazing in Ecuador

A bamboo forest like the one in Ecuador, a country in South America

Before the family planted bamboo along the river, their land was in poor shape. Many cattle had grazed there. They ate a lot of plants. This left the ground mostly bare. As a result, the banks of the river eroded. The river spilled onto the land. This left the land almost unusable.

Erosion is caused by people, animals, wind, or water wearing away the soil or land.

After the family planted bamboo along the river, everything changed. Bamboo has shallow roots that spread out over a wide area. It helped that bamboo is one of the fastest-growing plants in the world! The roots held the soil in place, stopping erosion. It also kept the river water clean. Many people in the area depend on the river for their water.

Bamboo roots don't grow deep. However, they cover a wide area.

These bamboo stems are like large straws.

A home built from bamboo

Also, the fallen bamboo leaves kept the ground moist. In addition, the bamboo the family planted has hollow stems. The stems can hold water. This can help during the dry season when there's little rain in Ecuador. Another big benefit is the family can **harvest** the bamboo and use it to build things. For the landowners, the bamboo is truly a miracle.

BAMBOO BASICS

There are around 1,450 types of bamboo in the world. Bamboo grows in hot **tropical** forests and on cold mountains. This **hardy** plant can be found across Asia, Australia, the Americas, and Africa. A few types even grow in the United States. The only place bamboo doesn't grow naturally is in Europe.

A bamboo forest in Asia

Bamboo belongs to a family of plants called grasses. It is an evergreen, keeping most of its leaves throughout the year. Some bamboos only grow 1 foot (0.3 m) high, while others soar to the sky. One kind from India can reach heights of more than 100 feet (30 m)! Others can grow 3 feet (0.9 m) wide. These types are known as giant bamboos.

Colorful bamboo

Bamboo comes in many colors. It ranges from yellow and pink to black and brown. Some bamboos even have stripes!

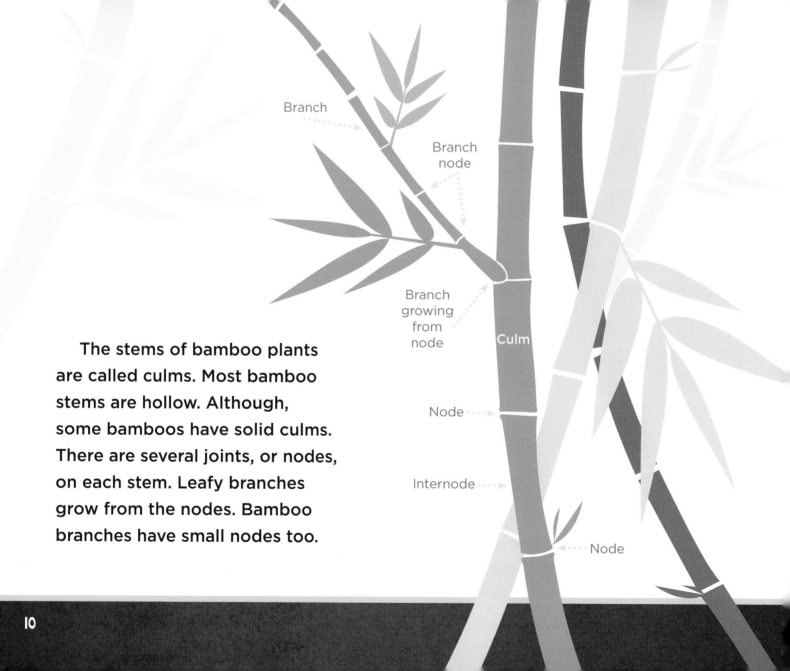

Branch

Branch node

Branch growing from node

Culm

Node

Internode

Node

The stems of bamboo plants are called culms. Most bamboo stems are hollow. Although, some bamboos have solid culms. There are several joints, or nodes, on each stem. Leafy branches grow from the nodes. Bamboo branches have small nodes too.

Flowering bamboo

A bamboo plant has a thick underground stem, or rhizome (RAHY-zohm). The rhizome is like the plant's aboveground stem. However, it grows roots and shoots instead of leaves and branches. Usually, the roots stay shallow. They don't grow more than 20 inches (51 cm) deep. Bamboos grow in two main ways: clumping and running. Clumping bamboos grow in big clusters and often spread slowly. Running bamboos spread far and fast.

It takes a long time for bamboos to flower and make seeds. For some bamboo species, this only happens after 65 to 120 years!

FAST GROWING

Some bamboos grow super-fast. A few types can spring up 3 feet (0.9 m) in one day! That's more than 1.5 inches (4 cm) in one hour. These kinds of bamboos can develop from a shoot to an adult plant in thirty days. However, most bamboos become adult plants in one to five years. After bamboo is harvested, it will continue to grow new shoots!

This bamboo shoot has recently popped out of the ground. Pests rarely attack bamboo. Therefore, it can be grown without chemicals.

Hardwood trees, like maples and oaks, can take thirty to forty years to **mature**. As these trees grow, their trunks widen over time. Bamboo is different. Bamboo culms stay the same thickness. After they're mature, they also never grow taller like trees.

Because many bamboo plants grow fast, they can be **destructive**. Without control, some running bamboos can quickly spread over a large area. Their rhizomes can send out hundreds of stems. They can smother **native** plants. Some can even damage property, such as sidewalks. There are places, like New York State, that ban certain running bamboos. These include golden and yellow grove bamboo.

However, there are simple ways to keep bamboo in check. Growers can place young bamboo plants in large pots to contain their roots. Or they can create an underground metal barrier to keep rhizomes from spreading. **Pruning** the rhizomes also helps keep bamboo from growing uncontrollably.

This bamboo is being grown in planters to keep its roots contained.

Some bamboos can grow wild if not controlled.

COUNTLESS USES

Bamboo bike

The benefits of bamboo outweigh any drawbacks. Why? Bamboo is very useful. For one thing, people can eat it! In China and other countries, bamboo shoots are cooked or **pickled**. The leaves can be brewed into tea. Bamboo also has **edible** seeds.

People also make things with bamboo. They grind up bamboo stems and press it into paper. One of the other uses of bamboo is cloth. Sheets, towels, and even socks can be made from bamboo **fibers**. Bamboo cloth is incredibly soft and **absorbent**.

Bamboo toothbrushes

Bamboo flooring

Soup with bamboo shoots

What else can people use bamboo for? Bamboo is a great replacement for wood! It's very strong, lightweight, and flexible. Bikes, cell phone cases, fishing rods, and even chopsticks can all be made from bamboo!

Bamboo chopsticks

Bamboo tea

Bamboo can help the environment too. Did you know that bamboo creates more oxygen than trees? Trees, bamboos, and most plants use **photosynthesis** to make their own food. First, they use sunlight to take in **carbon dioxide** and water. They turn these things into food and **oxygen**! Then plants release oxygen into the air.

Humans and other animals need oxygen to survive.

Bamboo is great at absorbing carbon dioxide and making oxygen. In fact, a bamboo forest releases thirty-five percent more oxygen than a tree forest. This makes bamboo a powerful tool to fight climate change.

When people burn fossil fuels in their cars or homes, carbon dioxide is released. Carbon dioxide traps heat in the air. The result is a warmer planet—and more extreme weather.

BUILDING WITH BAMBOO

Bamboo has even more uses on a construction site. Because of its strength, workers use bamboo to make scaffolding. Scaffolding is a tall platform. It's used to construct or repair the outside of a building. To make bamboo scaffolding, large and small stems are lashed together. In Hong Kong, soaring skyscrapers are built with bamboo scaffolding!

Bamboo scaffolding on a large building

In Asia, bamboo is plentiful. There, people have used it as a building material for thousands of years! Today, workers still construct bridges and houses out of bamboo. Bamboo can be easily split and bent. Therefore, it can be made into almost any size or shape. When split into strips, bamboo can be turned into **durable** flooring. Even thinner strips can be woven into chairs and other furniture.

A bamboo bridge over a river in Java, Indonesia

In Asia, people use hollow bamboo stems for water pipes!

ANIMALS AND BAMBOO

While humans don't need bamboo to survive, some animals do. Giant pandas live in the misty mountains of southern China. These black-and-white animals feed almost entirely on bamboo. They spend twelve hours per day eating the plant. An adult panda can eat 80 pounds (36 kg) of bamboo in one day!

Pandas use their teeth to peel off the hard outer layer of bamboo. Then they chew the softer inner layer with their flat back teeth. Pandas also eat bamboo leaves. First, they strip the leaves off the stem. Then they wad them up and gobble them down. Giant pandas may be the most famous bamboo eaters, but they're not the only ones.

A giant panda feasting on bamboo

Giant pandas are a kind of bear. Because they eat a lot, they poop a lot—up to 50 times a day!

The bamboo lemur of Madagascar also depends on bamboo. Lemurs live only in Madagascar. These furry creatures are related to monkeys. Most have long tails and big eyes. Bamboo lemurs eat mostly one type of bamboo.

Africa's golden monkey is yet another bamboo lover. It lives in the mountains of Central Africa. This monkey has a yellow patch on its back. Although it also eats fruit, bamboo is its main food. Mountain gorillas in Central Africa also like to eat bamboo.

This species is known as a golden bamboo lemur. It's about the size of a cat.

The golden monkey lives in Central Africa.

Only around 1,000 mountain gorillas are left in the wild. They're at serious risk of dying out.

Like people, mountain gorillas prefer munching on tender bamboo shoots. In fact, they'll travel far to find and feast on the shoots. However, the places where these amazing animals call home are disappearing. People are destroying bamboo forests to build farms, homes, and businesses.

Madagascar is a banana-shaped island in the Indian Ocean near Africa. In recent years, lemurs have seen ninety percent of their forest home disappear.

A WORLD WITHOUT BAMBOO

What if there were no bamboo? To start, the animals that depend on bamboo could die. This includes giant pandas and bamboo lemurs. People would have to find other sources for bamboo products. More slow-growing trees would likely be cut down. Plus, more land could erode. Also, people would lose a powerful weapon against climate change.

All hope is not lost. People can help save bamboo forests. Or they can help plant new ones! One of the most amazing things about bamboo is how quickly it grows. For this alone, bamboo may be a miracle plant.

This bamboo forest is in Japan.

BUILD WITH BAMBOO!

Bamboo is easy to build with. Use bamboo to make a pencil holder that's good for the planet—and you. You'll never have to go searching for a pencil again!

- Get a cardboard toilet paper tube, string, and glue. Then ask an adult to buy dried bamboo stakes at a craft or garden store.

- Ask the adult to trim the bamboo so each piece is 5 inches (13 cm) long. You will need ten to fifteen pieces.

- Apply glue sparingly to each piece of bamboo. Then stick the bamboo around the cardboard tube.

- Tie the string around the outside of your pencil holder until the glue dries. Then remove the string.

STICK YOUR PENCILS IN YOUR NEW BAMBOO PENCIL HOLDER. HAPPY WRITING!

GLOSSARY

absorbent (ab-ZORB-uhnt): able to soak up something.

carbon dioxide (KAR-buhn dye-AHK-side): a colorless and odorless gas given off when things decay or are burned.

climate change (KLYE-mit CHAYNJ): the warming of Earth's air and oceans due to environmental changes, such as a buildup of greenhouse gases that trap the sun's heat in Earth's atmosphere.

destructive (dih-STRUHK-tiv): tending to destroy.

durable (DUR-uh-buhl): able to last for a long time.

edible (ED-uh-buhl): able to be eaten.

eroded (ih-ROHD-uhd): worn away.

fibers (FYE-burz): threadlike structures.

fossil fuels (FOSS-uhl FYOOLZ): coal, oil, and gas made from the remains of plants and animals that died millions of years ago.

hardy (HAHR-dee): capable of withstanding cold, heat, or drought, for example.

harvest (HAR-vist): the gathering of plants that are ready to be used.

mature (muh-CHUR): to become fully grown.

native (NAY-tiv): belonging in a place.

oxygen (AWK-suh-juhn): an invisible gas found in water or air, which people and animals breathe.

photosynthesis (foh-tuh-SIN-thuh-siss): the making of food by plants using water, carbon dioxide, and sunlight.

pickled (PIK-uhld): preserved in a liquid.

pruning (PROON-ing): cutting back.

species (SPEE-sheez): types of animals or plants.

tropical (TROP-i-kuhl): having to do with the warm areas of Earth near the equator.

FOR MORE INFORMATION

Books

Jose, Dr. Sarah. *Trees, Leaves, Flowers, and Seeds*. New York, NY: DK Smithsonian, 2019.
Readers will learn fascinating facts about plants.

Lundgren, Julie. *Life Cycles: Bamboo*. Vero Beach, FL: Rourke Publishing, 2010.
This book explores the life cycle of bamboo.

Owen, Ruth. *Let's Investigate Plant Parts: Roots, Stems, Leaves, and Flowers*. New York, NY: Ruby Tuesday Books, 2017.
Read this book to learn about the basic structure of plants.

Websites

Brooklyn Botanic Garden: Bamboo
(https://www.bbg.org/gardening/article/bamboo)
Find out basics, including how to grow bamboo.

Missouri Botanical Garden: Controlling Bamboo
(https://www.missouribotanicalgarden.org/gardens-gardening/your-garden/help-for-thehome-gardener/advice-tips-resources/pests-and-problems/weeds/bamboo.aspx)
Learn about clumping and running bamboos.

San Diego Botanic Garden: Bamboo Garden
(https://www.sdbgarden.org/garden_bamboo.htm)
Readers can learn about the nation's biggest collection of bamboo.

INDEX

ABOUT THE AUTHOR

Joyce Markovics has written hundreds of books for kids. She's wild about plants, especially weird ones. Joyce lives in an old, creaky house along the Hudson River. She hopes the readers of this book will take action—in small and big ways—to protect nature, one of our greatest gifts. Joyce dedicates this book to her bamboo-loving brother, Bill, who's also a green warrior.